Famous Children

HANDEL

ANN RACHLIN
ILLUSTRATED BY SUSAN HELLARD

BARRON'S

It was 1692 and George was going to be seven years old tomorrow. Aunt Anna took him into town to choose a birthday present.

"Come on, George," she said, "let's go into that toyshop over there! I want to buy you something for your birthday."

"No, thank you, Aunt Anna. You know all I want is a musical instrument."

"And you know very well that your father will not allow a musical instrument in the house! Look there's my favorite pastry shop. We could buy some chocolate cake."

"No, thank you," answered George sadly.

George went home and put himself to bed. What a miserable start to a seventh birthday! He hadn't been asleep for long when he awoke. Someone was patting him on the shoulder. It was Aunt Anna.

"Ssh, George, don't make a sound! Follow me! I have a surprise for you!"

And so they crept up the stairs to the attic.

When they reached the attic door, Aunt Anna opened it and George stared inside in astonishment. There, standing on its slender legs, was the most beautiful clavier George had ever seen.

"But how on earth did you manage it?" George exclaimed.

"Never mind that," said Aunt Anna. "Aren't you going to try it?"

George Handel sat down on the stool and gazed at the keys. He was breathless with excitement. Then he began to run his fingers over the keyboard.

"Oh, Aunt Anna," said George, "thank you. This is the very best birthday present in the whole world!"

"I knew you would like it," said Aunt Anna, "but remember, practice when your father's out! You know he doesn't approve of music."

George's father was a barber-surgeon. Not only was he good at cutting hair, but he was also a doctor who could perform operations. Because he was a capable doctor, he had a very good job. He worked for the Duke of Weissenfels who loved music and had his own orchestra.

"Please, Father," begged George, "take me to meet the players in the orchestra! I'd love to talk to some real musicians!"

But Father Handel frowned and said,

"Books! Study! That's what's important! Not music!"

So George would wait until his father was out. Then he would race up to the attic to his own secret clavier and sit down and practice. He was so talented that without a single lesson he became a very good little musician.

"But how can I get to Weissenfels and meet some real musicians?" he wondered.

Every month, Father Handel would spend several days at Weissenfels, to trim the Duke's hair and to perform his operations. One fine morning, George woke up and heard his father moving around upstairs.

"He's going to Weissenfels! I know he is! Maybe he'll let me go with him this time!" He jumped out of bed and got dressed.

Upstairs, his father finished packing his scissors and special instruments. When he came downstairs with his bag, George was waiting.

"Father, please may I go to Weissenfels with you?"

"No!" said his father. "Books! Not music! You must study hard!" And he walked quickly across the courtyard and climbed into the coach.

The coach started off across the cobblestones. But George made up his mind. He *would* go with his father. He started to run after the coach. Before very long, the coachman reported to Father Handel that there was a little boy following them. Father Handel looked around. He saw George and gave orders for the coach to stop.

George came panting up in a cloud of dust and looked up into his father's angry face. His father shook his finger and said,

"Now, then, George, you were wrong to disobey, but it's too far to go back! Climb up, but when we get to Weissenfels you had better behave yourself."

"Yes, Father," said George meekly. He climbed aboard the coach. He was happy. He'd gotten his own way! He was going to Weissenfels to meet those musicians at last.

Every morning, while the Duke held his court and Father Handel saw his patients, George would climb up to the organ loft in the Duke's chapel and sit down and play. One day, the organist found him and said,

"You play well! Where did you study?"

"I have never had any lessons, Sir," said George.

"No lessons? Really? Well you'd better be here next Sunday when the Duke comes to the service."

On Sunday morning, the Duke of Weissenfels attended his chapel to pray. George was up in the organ loft, staring down.

"Oh, look! Look at all those people! Look at the ladies all dressed up in such beautiful clothes! Look at the gentlemen's wigs! They're all so grand."

"**N**ow, young man," said the organist, "you are going to play the march when the Duke stands up at the end of the service!"

"Me? You must be joking!" said George.

"Not a joke," said the organist. "I mean it. You will play the march at the end of the service."

"But how will I know when to start?"

"I told you," said the organist, "when the Duke stands up."

George was scared. What if the Duke was angry? A little boy, playing the march at the end of the service? It was unheard of!

He peeked over the edge. There was the Duke of Weissenfels, looking very strict! George turned around and sat down. The service was nearly over. His hands were trembling. He waited for that magic moment when the Duke of Weissenfels would stand up at the end of the service.

There was a moment of silence... and then the Duke of Weissenfels stood up! Everyone rose as the Duke went solemnly down the aisle. One lady was just beginning her curtsy, when she noticed little George playing the organ. She was so surprised that she wobbled! Then the next lady looked up and saw him too, and *she* wobbled!

The Duke frowned at the wobbling ladies, and followed their gaze.

"A boy?" he said. "Who is that boy?"

"That is the son of your barber-surgeon, Mr. Handel, Sir."

"Is he indeed? Send Mr. Handel to me, with the boy."

Father Handel bowed before the Duke.

"A very fine little musician you have there, Mr. Handel."

"Well, he's not bad!" said Father Handel.

"Not bad? He's very good! Who's his teacher?"

"Oh, he's not taking lessons, Your Grace," replied Father Handel.

"What?" cried the Duke. "He should be studying. Here you are, boy!" and he gave George a purse of golden coins.

"You must have music lessons!" he said. "Mr. Zachau is a fine teacher." Father Handel could not refuse! As soon as they arrived back home, George rushed to tell Aunt Anna his good news.

"I'm going to have music lessons! The Duke says so! Now we don't have to keep the clavier a secret anymore!"

George Frederic Handel studied hard and became a famous composer whose music is known and played all over the world. He was the favorite musician of King George I and King George II of England, where he lived most of his life. He loved to write music about Bible stories, called "oratorios." One of them, "The Messiah," is probably his best-loved work.